亨利和玛可

第一本书

【美】辛西娅·赖蓝特／著
【美】苏西·史蒂文森／绘
安慎／译

大连理工大学出版社

本书由大连理工大学出版社独家出版
著作权合同登记 06-2014 年第 132 号

图书在版编目（CIP）数据

第一本书：英、汉 / (美) 赖蓝特, (美) 史蒂文森著 ; 安慎译. —大连 :大连理工大学出版社, 2015.1
（亨利和玛奇）
ISBN 978-7-5611-9662-5

Ⅰ. ①第… Ⅱ. ①赖… ②史… ③安… Ⅲ. ①儿童文学-图画故事-美国-现代 Ⅳ. ①I712.85

中国版本图书馆CIP数据核字(2014)第284384号

大连理工大学出版社出版
地址：大连市软件园路 80 号　邮政编码：116023
发行：0411-84708842　传真：0411-84701466　邮购：0411-84708943
E-mail:dutp@dutp.cn　URL:http://www.dutp.cn
大连住友彩色印刷有限公司印刷　大连理工大学出版社发行

幅面尺寸：152mm × 228mm　印张：3　字数：38 千字
2015 年 1 月第 1 版　2015 年 1 月第 1 次印刷

责任编辑：陈　玫　责任校对：刘　强
封面设计：宋善怡

ISBN 978-7-5611-9662-5　定　价：10.80 元

CONTENTS

Henry

Henry had no brothers
and no sisters.
"I want a brother,"
he told his parents.
"Sorry," they said.
Henry had no friends
on his street.

"I want to live
on a different street,"
he told his parents.
"Sorry," they said.
Henry had no pets
at home.
"I want to have a dog,"
he told his parents.
"Sorry," they almost said.

But first they looked
at their house
with no brothers and sisters.
Then they looked
at their street
with no children.
Then they looked
at Henry's face.

Then they looked at each other.
"Okay," they said.
"I want to hug you!"
Henry told his parents.
And he did.

Mudge

Henry searched for a dog.

"Not just any dog," said Henry.

"Not a short one," he said.

"Not a curly one," he said.

"And no pointed ears."

Then he found Mudge.
Mudge had floppy ears,
not pointed.
And Mudge had straight fur,
not curly.
But Mudge was short.
“Because he’s a puppy,”
Henry said.
“He’ll grow.”

And did he ever!

He grew out of his puppy cage.

He grew out of his dog cage.

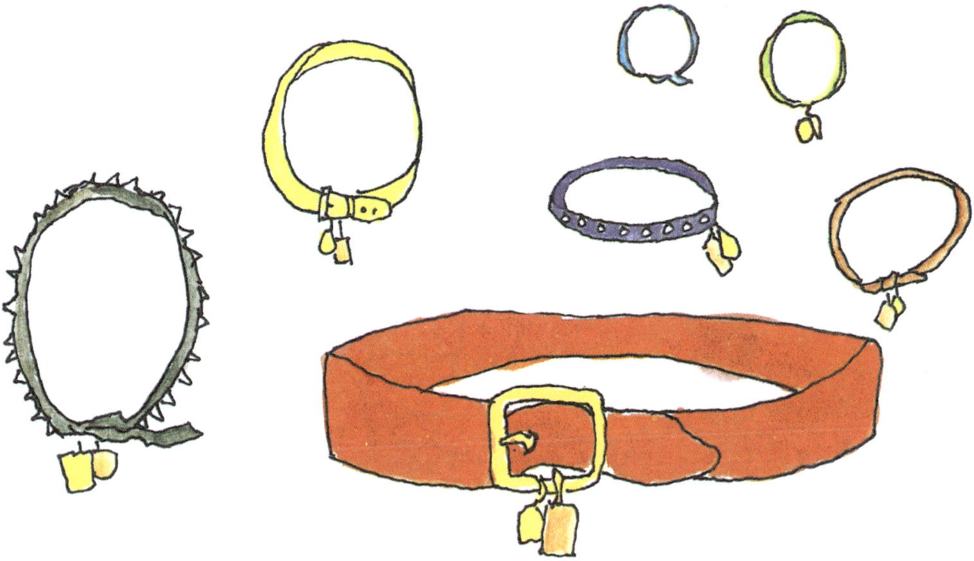

He grew out of seven collars

in a row.

And when he finally

stopped growing…

He weighed one hundred eighty pounds,
he stood three feet tall,
and he drooled.
“I’m glad you’re not short,”
Henry said.

And Mudge licked him,
then sat on him.

Henry

Henry used to walk
to school alone.
When he walked
he used to worry about
tornadoes,
ghosts,
biting dogs,
and bullies.

He walked as fast
as he could.
He looked straight ahead.
He never looked back.
But now he walked to school
with Mudge.

And now when he walked,
he thought about
vanilla ice cream,
rain,
rocks,
and good dreams,
He walked to school
but not too fast.
He walked to school
and sometimes backward.

He walked to school
and patted Mudge's big head,
happy.

Mudge

Mudge loved Henry's room.
He loved the dirty socks.
He loved the stuffed bear.
He loved the fish tank.
But mostly he loved Henry's bed.

Because in Henry's bed
was Henry.
Mudge loved to climb in
with Henry.
Then he loved
to smell him.

He smelled his lemon hair.
He smelled his milky mouth.
He smelled his soapy ears.
He smelled his chocolate fingers.

Then he put his head
by Henry's head.
He looked at the fish tank.
He looked at the bear.
He looked at Henry.
He licked him.
And he fell asleelp.

One day Mudge took a walk
without Henry.
The sun was shining,
the birds were flying,
the grass smelled sweet.
Mudge couldn't wait for Henry.
So he left.

He went down one road,
sniffling the bushes,
then down another road,
kicking up dust.
He went through a field,
across a stream,
into some pine trees.

And when he came out
on the other side,
he was lost.

He couldn’t smell Henry.
He couldn’t smell
his front porch.
He couldn’t smell
the street he lived on.
Mudge looked all around
and didn’t see anything
or anyone
he knew.

He whined a little,
alone without Henry.
Then he lay down,
alone without Henry.
He missed Henry's bed.

Henry thought Mudge
would be with him always.
He thought Mudge
made everything safe.
He thought Mudge
would never go away.

And when Mudge did go away,
when Henry called and called
but Mudge didn't come,
Henry's heart hurt
and he cried for an hour.
But when he finished crying,
Henry said, "Mudge loves me.
He wouldn't leave.
He must be lost."

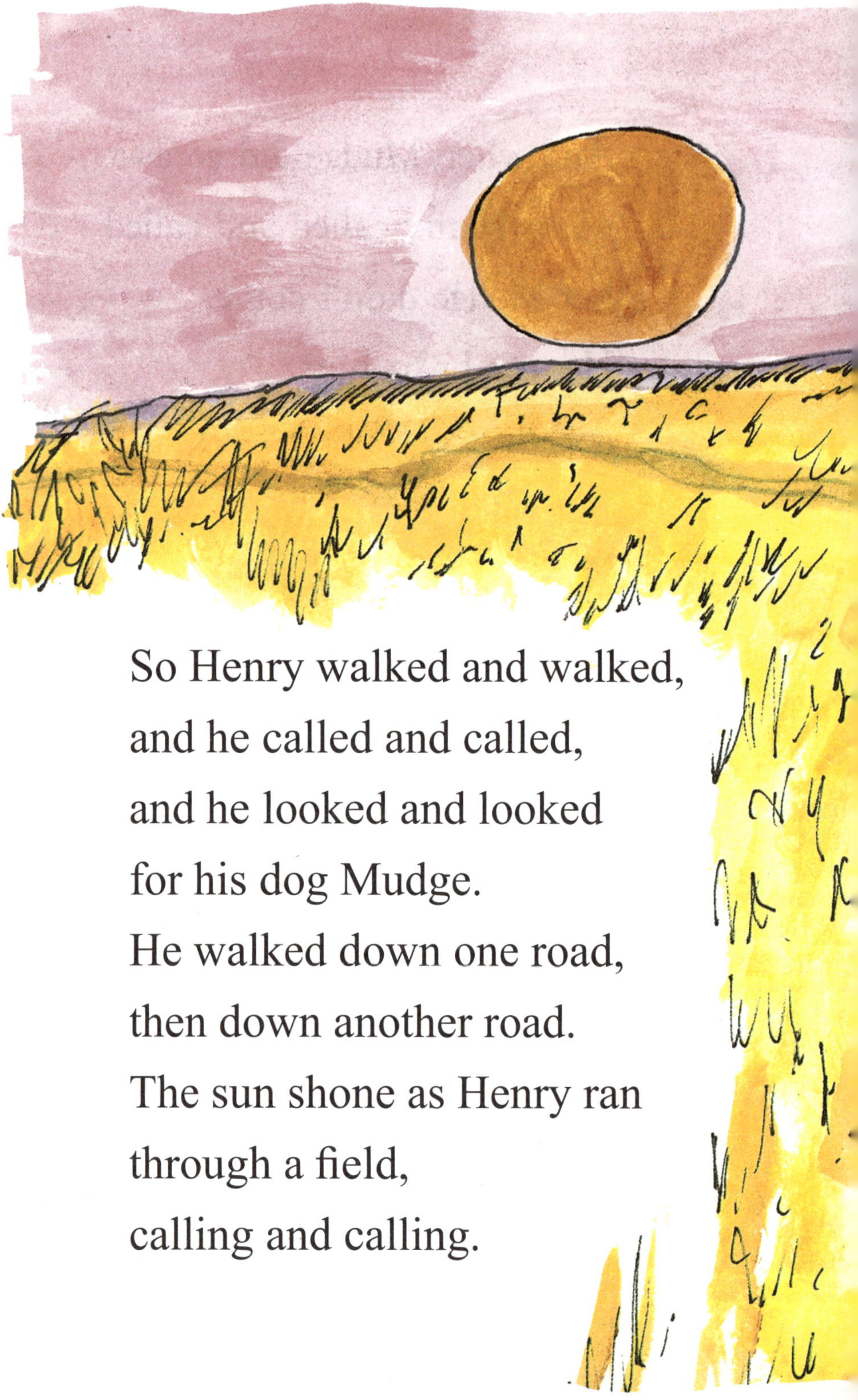

So Henry walked and walked,
and he called and called,
and he looked and looked
for his dog Mudge.
He walked down one road,
then down another road.
The sun shone as Henry ran
through a field,
calling and calling.

The birds flew past
as he stood beside a stream,
calling and calling.

And the tears fell again
as he looked at the
empty pine trees
for his lost dog.
"Mudge!" he called, one last time.

And Mudge woke up
from his lonely sleep,
then
came
running.

Henry and Mudge

Every day when Henry woke up,
he saw Mudge's big head.
And every day
when Mudge woke up,
he saw Henry's small face.

They ate breakfast
at the same time;

they ate supper
at the same time.

And when Henry was at school,
Mudge just lay around
and waited.
Mudge never went for a walk
without Henry again.
And Henry never worried
that Mudge would leave.

Because sometimes, in their dreams,
they saw long silent roads,
big wide fields,
deep streams,
and pine trees.

In those dreams,
Mudge was alone
and Henry was alone.
So when Mudge woke up
and knew Henry was with him,
he remembered the dream
and stayed closer.

And when Henry woke up
and knew Mudge was with him,
he remembered the dream
and the looking
and the calling
and the fear
and he knew
he would never lose Mudge again.

亨利

亨利没有兄弟和姐妹。

“我想有个弟弟。”他对父母说。

“对不起。”他们回答道。

亨利在所住的街区没有朋友。

“我想住在其他的街区。”他对父母说。

“对不起。”他们说。

亨利家没有宠物。

“我想养条狗。”他对父母说。

他们差点要回答说：“对不起，不行。”

但是他们先看了看没有兄弟姐妹的家，再看看没有小孩儿的街区，最后看了看亨利的脸。两个人相互看了一眼，异口同声地说：“没问题！”

“太好了！”亨利扑向爸爸妈妈，一家人高兴地拥抱在一起。

玛奇

亨利开始琢磨该选一条什么样儿的狗。

“不是什么狗我都喜欢，”他说，“不能个头小，不能是卷毛的，也不能是尖耳朵。”

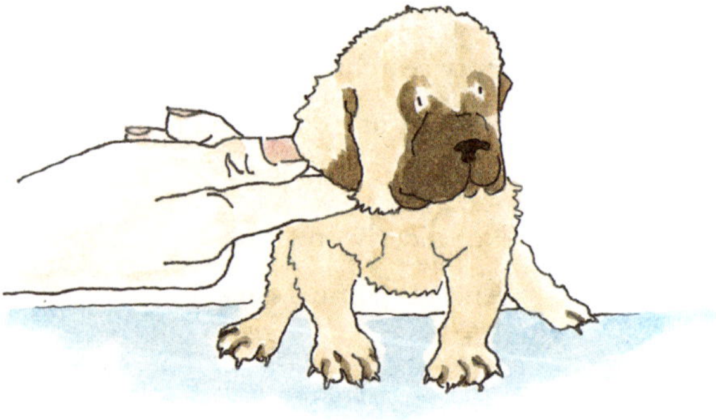

于是，他发现了“玛奇”。

玛奇的耳朵软软的，不是尖尖的。玛奇的毛是直的，不是卷的，但是玛奇的个头小。“因为他是一只小狗，”亨利说，“他会长大的。”

玛奇的确长大了！

小笼子很快住不下玛奇了，大笼子很快也住不下玛奇了。

当玛奇接连用坏了七个项圈以后，他终于不再长了。

他有一百八十磅重，站起来有三尺高，还流着口水。“我很高兴你不再是小个子啦。”亨利说。玛奇舔了舔他，坐在了亨利的身上。

亨利

以前亨利一个人步行去上学。

他一边走一边担心，

会不会有龙卷风啊？

会不会有妖怪啊？

会不会有咬人的狗啊？

会不会有恶霸啊？

他能走多快就走多快，径直看着前方，从来不往后看。

现在，他可以和玛奇一起去上学。

一边走着一边想的是香草味的冰淇淋，雨滴，棒棒糖还有美梦。

他朝学校走去，但不是很快。

他朝学校走去，但有时倒着走。

他朝学校走去，拍着玛奇的大脑壳，真幸福。

玛奇

玛奇喜欢亨利的房间。

他喜欢脏袜子，喜欢玩具熊，喜欢鱼缸。

他最喜欢亨利的床，因为在床上的是亨利。

玛奇喜欢爬上床和亨利待在一起，喜欢闻亨利的味道。

他闻闻亨利柠檬色的头发，闻闻他奶香味的小嘴，闻闻他肥皂香的耳朵，闻闻他沾满巧克力味道的小手……接着把自己的脑袋紧挨着亨利的脑袋，看看鱼缸、看看玩具熊、舔舔亨利，然后进入了梦乡。

玛奇

一天，玛奇出去散步，但没和亨利一起。阳光明媚，草长莺飞，玛奇没有等亨利，便自己离开了。

他边嗅着灌木丛边沿着路往前走，然后又扬起一阵尘土顺着另一条路往前走。

他越过田野，穿过河流，来到一片松林里。

当从松林的另一边出来时，他迷路了。

他闻不到亨利，闻不到家里的前厅，闻不到所在的街区。玛奇朝周围看了看，看不见任何熟悉的人或事。

他呜呜地叫了一会儿，没有亨利在身边。

他独自躺了下来，没有亨利在身边。

他想念亨利的小床。

亨利

亨利认为玛奇会一直跟他待在一起，认为玛奇每件事都做得很稳妥，认为玛奇不会自己乱跑。

当玛奇的的确确跑开的时候，当亨利不停地呼喊但是玛奇依然不出现的时候，亨利伤心了，哭了一个多小时。哭过以后，亨利说：“玛奇喜欢我，他不会离开我，一定是迷路了。”

于是亨利不停地走，不停地喊，不停地寻找着他的玛奇。他顺着一条路找，然后又沿着另一条路找。

顶着炎炎烈日，亨利跑过田野，不断地呼喊。

伴着鸟儿飞过，亨利站在小河边，不停地呼喊。

当他在空荡荡的松林里寻找着走失的玛奇时，泪水再次落下来。

“玛奇！”亨利最后一次大声呼喊。

玛奇从孤单的睡梦中醒来，循声狂奔。

亨利和玛奇

每天亨利醒来时，他就能看见玛奇的大脑壳。

每天玛奇醒来时，他就能看见亨利的小脸蛋。

他们一起吃早饭，一起吃晚饭。

亨利在学校上课的时候，玛奇就躺在那儿等他。

如果亨利不在身边，玛奇就再也不去散步了。

亨利再也不担心玛奇走失了。

有时在梦里，他们看到漫长的寂静的道路，广阔无垠的田野，深不见底的河流还有松树林。在这些梦里，玛奇独自一人，亨利也是独自一人。当玛奇醒来，知道亨利和自己在一起的时候，他想起了做的梦，所以更靠近亨利了。

当亨利醒来，知道玛奇和自己在一起的时候，他想起了做的梦，想起了寻找、呼喊和恐惧。他知道自己再也不能让玛奇走丢了。